STUDYING GENDER IN CLASSICAL ANTIQUITY

This book investigates how varying practices of gender shaped people's lives and experiences across the societies of ancient Greece and Rome. Exploring how gender was linked with other socio-political characteristics such as wealth, status, age and life stage, as well as with individual choices, in the very different world of classical antiquity is fascinating in its own right. But later perceptions of ancient literature and art have profoundly influenced the development of gendered ideologies and hierarchies in the West, and influenced the study of gender itself. Questioning how best to untangle and interpret difficult sources is a key aim. This book exploits a wide range of archaeological, material cultural, visual, spatial, demographic, epigraphical and literary evidence to consider households, families, life cycles and the engendering of time, legal and political institutions, beliefs about bodies, sex and sexuality, gender and space, the economic implications of engendered practices, and gender in religion and magic.

LIN FOXHALL is Professor of Greek Archaeology and History at the University of Leicester. She has worked in Greece and Southern Italy and currently co-directs a field project in Calabria. She has written extensively on agriculture, land use and gender in classical antiquity. Her publications include *Olive Cultivation in Ancient Greece: Seeking the Ancient Economy* (2007), two books on masculinity edited with John Salmon, *Thinking Men: Masculinity and its Self-Representation in the Classical Tradition* and *When Men were Men: Masculinity, Power and Identity in Classical Antiquity* (1998), as well as *Money, Labour and Land: Approaches to the Economics of Ancient Greece* (2002), edited with Paul Cartledge and Edward Cohen.

KEY THEMES IN ANCIENT HISTORY

EDITORS

P. A. Cartledge
Clare College, Cambridge

P. D. A. Garnsey
Jesus College, Cambridge

Key Themes in Ancient History aims to provide readable, informed and original studies of various basic topics, designed in the first instance for students and teachers of Classics and Ancient History, but also for those engaged in related disciplines. Each volume is devoted to a general theme in Greek, Roman or, where appropriate, Graeco-Roman history, or to some salient aspect or aspects of it. Besides indicating the state of current research in the relevant area, authors seek to show how the theme is significant for our own as well as ancient culture and society. By providing books for courses that are oriented around themes it is hoped to encourage and stimulate promising new developments in teaching and research in ancient history.

Other books in the series

Death-ritual and Social Structure in Classical Antiquity, by Ian Morris
978 0 521 37465 1 (hardback) 978 0 521 37611 2 (paperback)

Literacy and Orality in Ancient Greece, by Rosalind Thomas
978 0 521 37346 3 (hardback) 978 0 521 37742 3 (paperback)

Slavery and Society at Rome, by Keith Bradley
978 0 521 37287 9 (hardback) 978 0 521 37887 1 (paperback)

Law, Violence, and Community in Classical Athens, by David Cohen
978 0 521 38167 3 (hardback) 978 0 521 38837 5 (paperback)

Public Order in Ancient Rome, by Wilfried Nippel
978 0 521 38327 1 (hardback) 978 0 521 38749 1 (paperback)

Friendship in the Classical World, by David Konstan
978 0 521 45402 5 (hardback) 978 0 521 45998 3 (paperback)

Sport and Society in Ancient Greece, by Mark Golden
978 0 521 49698 8 (hardback) 978 0 521 49790 9 (paperback)

Food and Society in Classical Antiquity, by Peter Garnsey
978 0 521 64182 1 (hardback) 978 0 521 64588 1 (paperback)

ways in which this was done was by the manipulation of time and space, so that activities that might clash along gender lines could be orchestrated by temporal sequence. Another way was by carving out legal and social niches in which 'unacceptable' practices such as prostitution could exist, even if they were then hedged with prohibitions.

I have also tried to highlight the diversity of gender in practice across the ancient classical world. In a short book like this one it is tempting to focus on the normative, and to cling to the well-established case studies, where our evidence is most abundant. To some extent I have certainly fallen into these traps. However, I have also tried to include evidence that offers perspectives on gender that go beyond the familiar literary texts, thereby setting those texts in a broader context. In particular I have tried to stress throughout the book that the very foundations of gendered behaviour, as well as its wider social contextualization, are substantially different in Roman societies than in Greek ones, even though there come to be many complex structural and ideological relationships between them.

For the Greeks and the Romans, gender was central to thought, behaviour, social conventions, politics, economics and ideals. In different ways, this holds for numerous other cultures and societies, including our own. Though we may encounter and address it in radically different ways in the modern world, the subject has lost none of its urgency since antiquity. Indeed, beliefs, representations and images of a wide range of gendered ideals and performance from the worlds of classical antiquity have provided much inspiration for later periods, and that legacy is inextricably embedded in our own thought-world today. And that, apart from its intrinsic fascination, is a good reason for studying gender in classical antiquity.

by Nevett 2010, and the more basic introduction to Greek houses by J. Morgan 2010. Important collections on houses and domestic space include Westgate *et al.* 2007; Ault and Nevett 2005; Laurence and Wallace-Hadrill 1997; Laurence and Newsome 2011. The most extensively studied houses and households in the ancient world have been those of Pompeii (Laurence 1994; Wallace-Hadrill 1994; Allison 2004).

Overviews of Greek athletics include S. Miller 2004; Kyle 2007; Newby 2006. On 'Greek' athletics in the Roman world see Newby 2005 and König 2005. On the roles of sex and sexuality in sport see Scanlon 2002. For the participation of women and girls in Greek athletics see Scanlon 1984; 1988; 2002; M. Dillon 2000; Serwint 1993.

The substantial literature on Roman bath buildings often neglects bathing practice; Delaine and Johnston 1999 is a notable exception. The most complete recent surveys on bathing with full bibliographies are Yegül 2010 and Fagan 1999.

7 RELIGION

A great deal has been written on women and religion, much more than on gender, or men, and religion. Useful works on women and (sometimes) gender in Greek religion include Larson 1995; Blundell and Williamson 1998; Calame 2001; M. Dillon 2002; Cole 2004; Georgoudi 2005; Connelly 2007. On young men and religion see Vidal-Naquet 1986, Kleijwegt 1991; Vernant 1991: 220–43. For general works on women and gender in Roman religion see Staples 1998; Schultz 2006; Takács 2008. The Vestal Virgins have long attracted a huge amount of interest although the scholarship varies in quality. The seminal work of modern times remains Beard 1980, but this has been supplemented by more recent studies including Staples 1998; H. Parker 2004; Wildfang 2006; Takács 2008. Much of the work on 'women's rites' is over-enthusiastic to draw connections across time and space in the ancient world, e.g. Vernant 1991: 195–219; Versnel 1992. On participation in or exclusion from cult on the basis of gender see David 2000; Schultz 2000; Dorcey 1989. On love magic and curses, Graf 1997; Faraone 1999; and Eidinow 2007 are key works, but see also Dickie 2000.

Bibliography

Allison, P. (1993) 'How do we identify the use of space in Roman housing?', in E. Moorman, ed., *Functional and Spatial Analysis of Wall Painting*: 1–8. Leiden.

(1997) 'Artefact distribution and spatial function in Pompeian houses', in Rawson and Weaver 1997: 321–54.

ed. (1999) *The Archaeology of Household Activities*. London and New York.

(2004) *Pompeian Households*. Los Angeles.

(2007) 'Engendering Roman domestic space', in Westgate *et al.* 2007: 343–50.

Alston, R. (1995) *Soldier and Society in Roman Egypt: a social history*. London and New York.

(1998) 'Arms and the man: soldiers, masculinity and power in Republican and Imperial Rome', in Foxhall and Salmon 1998b : 205–23.

Anderson, J. (2012) *Gestures, Postures and Body Actions: body language in Hellenistic art and society*. Oxford.

Arthur, M. (1973) 'Early Greece: the origins of the western attitude toward women', *Arethusa* 6: 7–58.

Ault, B. and Nevett, L. eds. (2005) *Ancient Greek Houses and Households*. Philadelphia.

Bachofen, J. (1975) *Das Mutterrecht: eine Untersuchung über die Gynaikokratie der alten Welt nach ihrer religiösen und rechtlichen Natur*. H.-J. Heinrichs, ed. Frankfurt.

Bagnall, R. S. and Frier, B. W. (1994) *The Demography of Roman Egypt*. Cambridge.

Balme, D. (1992) *Aristotle's de Partibus animalium I and de Generatione animalium I*. Oxford.

Balsdon, D. (1974) *Roman Women: their history and habits*. Rev. edn. London.

Baltrusch, E. (1989) *Regimen morum: die Reglementierung des Privatlebens der Senatoren und Ritter der römischen Republik und frühen Kaiserzeit*. Munich.

Barát, E. (2009) 'The troubling internet space of "woman's mind"', *Discourse and Communication* 3: 401–26.

Barber, E. (1992) 'The peplos of Athena', in Neils 1992b: 103–17.

(1994) *Women's Work: the first 20,000 years. Women, cloth and society in early times*. New York and London.

Cohen, A. and Rutter, J., eds. (2007) *Constructions of Childhood in Ancient Greece and Italy. Hesperia Suppl.* 41. Princeton.

Cohen, D. (1990) 'The social context of adultery at Athens', in P. A. Cartledge, P. C. Millett and S. C. Todd, eds., *Nomos: essays in Athenian law, politics and society*: 147–65. Cambridge.

(1991) *Law, Sexuality and Society: the enforcement of morals in classical Athens.* Cambridge.

Cohen, E. (2003) *The Athenian Nation.* Princeton.

(2006) 'Free and unfree sexual work: an economic analysis of Athenian prostitution', in Faraone and McClure 2006: 95–124.

Cole, S. (2004) *Landscapes, Gender and Ritual Space: the ancient Greek experience.* Berkeley.

Coleman, K. (forthcoming) *Q. Sulpicius Maximus, Poet, Eleven Years Old.* Ann Arbor, MI.

Connelly, J. (2007) *Portrait of a Priestess: women and ritual in ancient Greece.* Princeton.

Cooper, K. (2007) *The Fall of the Roman Household.* Cambridge.

Corbier, M. (2001) 'Child exposure and abandonment', in Dixon 2001: 52–73.

Cotton, H. and Greenfield, J. (1994) 'Babatha's property and the law of succession in the Babatha archive', *Zeitschrift für Papyrologie und Epigraphik* 104: 211–24.

Coucouzeli, A. (2007) 'From megaron to *oikos* at Zagora', in Westgate *et al.* 2007: 169–81.

Coulton, J. (1976) *The Architectural Development of the Greek Stoa.* Oxford.

Cox, C. A. (1998) *Household Interests: property, marriage strategies and family dynamics in ancient Athens.* Princeton.

Crook, J. A. (1967) *Law and Life of Rome.* London.

Crowe, F. (2001) 'Women, burial data and issues of inclusion: the problems and potential of Romano-British cemeteries', in Dixon 2001: 144–62.

Crowe, F., Sperduti, A., O'Connell, T., Craig, O., Kirsanow, K., Germoni, P., Macchiarelli, R., Garnsey, P. and Bondoli, P. (2010) 'Water-related occupations and diet in two Roman coastal communities (Italy, first to third century AD): correlation between stable carbon and nitrogen isotope values and auricular exostosis prevalence', *American Journal of Physical Anthropology* 142: 355–66.

Culham, P. (1986) 'Again: what meaning lies in colour!', *Zeitschrift für Papyrologie und Epigraphik* 64: 235–45.

Daniel, R. and Maltomini, F. (1990–2) *Supplementum magicum.* Dusseldorf.

Dasen, V. and Späth, T., eds. (2010) *Children, Memory and Family Identity in Roman Culture.* Oxford.

David, J. (2000) 'The exclusion of women in the Mithraic mysteries: ancient or modern?', *Numen* 47: 121–41.

Davidson, J. (1997) *Courtesans and Fishcakes: the consuming passions of classical Athens.* London.

(2006) 'Revolutions in human time', in S. Goldhill and R. Osborne, eds., *Rethinking Revolutions through Ancient Greece*: 29–67. Cambridge.

(2007) *The Greeks and Greek Love*. London.

(2011) 'Bodymaps: sexing space and zoning gender in ancient Athens', *Gender & History* 23: 597–614.

Davies, J. K. (1971) *Athenian Propertied Families 600–300 BC*. Oxford.

Dawkins, R. M., ed. (1929) *The Sanctuary of Artemis Orthia at Sparta*. London.

de Beauvoir, S. (1953) *The Second Sex*. Tr. H. M. Parshley. London. Originally published in 1949 as *Le deuxième sexe*, Paris.

de Cazanove, O. (1987) 'L'incapacité sacrificielle des femmes à Rome (à propos de Plutarque *Quaest. Rom.* 85)', *Phoenix* 41: 159–73.

de Grazia, C. and Williams, C. K. (1977) 'Corinth 1976: Forum Southwest', *Hesperia* 46: 40–81.

de Ste Croix, G. (1970) 'Some observations on the property rights of Athenian women', *Classical Review* 20: 273–8.

Dean-Jones, L. (1991) 'The cultural construct of the female body in classical Greek science', in Pomeroy 1991: 111–37.

(1994) *Women's Bodies in Classical Greek Science*. Oxford.

Delaine, J. and Johnston, D., eds. (1999) *Roman Baths and Bathing*. Portsmouth, RI.

Des Bouvrie, S. (1984) 'Augustus' legislation on morals – which morals and what aims?', *Symbolae Osloenses* 59: 93–113.

Detel, W. (2005) *Foucault and Classical Antiquity: power, ethics and knowledge*. Cambridge.

Detienne, M. (1989) 'The violence of well-born ladies', in M. Detienne and J.-P. Vernant, eds., *The Cuisine of Sacrifice among the Greeks*: 129–47. Tr. M. Muellner. Chicago and London. Originally published in 1979 as *La cuisine du sacrifice en pays grec*. Paris.

Devereux, G. (1970) 'The nature of Sappho's seizure in fr. 31 LP as evidence of her inversion', *Classical Quarterly* 20: 17–31.

Dickie, M. (2000) 'Who practised love-magic in classical antiquity and in the late Roman world?', *Classical Quarterly* 50: 563–83.

Diddle Uzzi, J. (2005) *Children in the Visual Arts of Imperial Rome*. Cambridge.

(2007) 'The power of parenthood in official Roman art', in Cohen and Rutter 2007: 61–81.

Dillon, M. (2000) 'Did *parthenoi* attend the Olympic Games? Girls and women competing, spectating and carrying out cult roles at Greek religious festivals', *Hermes* 128: 457–80.

(2002) *Girls and Women in Classical Greek Religion*. London and New York.

Dillon, S. (2006) *Ancient Greek Portrait Sculpture*. Cambridge.

(2010) *The Female Portrait Statue in the Greek World*. Cambridge.

Dixon, S. (1992) *The Roman Family*. Baltimore and London.

(1997) 'Conflict in the Roman family', in Rawson and Weaver 1997: 149–68.

ed. (2001) *Childhood, Class and Kin in the Roman World*. London and New York.

Dorcey, P. (1989) 'The role of women in the cult of Silvanus', *Numen* 36: 143–55.

Dover, K. (1989) *Greek Homosexuality*. 2nd edn. London (1st edn 1978).

Drees, L. (1967) *Olympia: gods, artists and athletes*. London.

Dunbar, R. and Barrett, L. (2007a) 'Evolutionary psychology in the round', in Dunbar and Barrett 2007b: 3–9.

eds. (2007b) *Oxford Handbook of Evolutionary Psychology*. Oxford.

Edmondson, J. (2008) 'Public dress and social control in late Republican and early Imperial Rome', in Edmondson and Keith 2008b: 21–46.

Edmondson, J. and Keith, A. (2008a) 'Introduction: from costume history to dress studies', in Edmondson and Keith 2008b: 1–17.

eds. (2008b) *Roman Dress and the Fabrics of Roman Culture*. Toronto, Buffalo and London.

Edwards, Catherine (1993) *The Politics of Immorality in Ancient Rome*. Cambridge.

Eidinow, E. (2007) *Oracles, Curses and Risk among the Ancient Greeks*. Oxford.

Elderkin, K. (1930) 'Jointed dolls in antiquity', *American Journal of Archaeology* 34: 455–79.

Engels, D. (1980) 'The problem of female infanticide in the Greco-Roman world', *Classical Philology* 75: 112–20.

Erker, D. (2011) 'Gender and Roman funeral ritual', in Hope and Huskinson 2011: 40–60.

Eschebach, H. (1979) *Die Stabianer Thermen in Pompeji*. Berlin.

Evans, A. (1902/1903) 'The Palace of Knossos: provisional report for the year 1903', *Annual of the British School at Athens* 9: 1–153.

(1921) *The Palace of Minos I*. London.

(1928) *The Palace of Minos II*. London.

(1930) *The Palace of Minos III*. London.

Fagan, G. (1999) *Bathing in Public in the Roman World*. Ann Arbor, MI.

(2002) 'Messalina's folly', *Classical Quarterly* 52: 566–79.

(2006) 'Bathing for health with Celsus and Pliny the Elder', *Classical Quarterly* 56: 190–207.

Faraone, C. A. (1991) 'The agonistic context of early Greek binding spells', in C. A. Faraone and D. Obbink, eds., *Magika hiera: ancient Greek magic and religion*: 3–32. Oxford.

(1999) *Ancient Greek Love Magic*. Cambridge, MA.

(2011) 'Magical and medical approaches to the wandering womb in the ancient Greek world', *Classical Antiquity* 30: 1–32.

Faraone, C. A. and McClure, L., eds. (2006) *Prostitutes and Courtesans in the Ancient World*. Madison, WI.

Ferrari, G. (2002) *Figures of Speech: men and maidens in ancient Greece*. Chicago.

Fisher, N. (1998) 'Gymnasia and the democratic values of leisure', in P. Cartledge, P. Millett and S. von Reden, eds., *Kosmos: essays on order, conflict and community in classical Athens*: 84–104. Cambridge.

Flemming, R. (1999) '*Quae corpore quaestum facit*: the sexual economy of female prostitution in the Roman Empire', *Journal of Roman Studies* 89: 38–61.

(2000) *Medicine and the Making of Roman Women: gender, nature, and authority from Celsus to Galen*. Oxford.

(2007) 'Festus and the role of women in Roman religion', in F. Glinister and C. Woods, eds., *Verrius, Festus and Paul: lexicography, scholarship and society*: 87–108. London.

(2007) 'Women, writing and medicine in the classical world', *Classical Quarterly* 57: 257–79.

Flower, H. (1996) *Ancestor Masks and Aristocratic Power in Roman Culture*. Oxford.

Fögen, T. and Lee, M., eds. (2009) *Bodies and Boundaries in Graeco-Roman Antiquity*. Berlin and New York.

Foley H. (2001) *Female Acts in Greek Tragedy*. Princeton.

Fornara, C. (1983) *Archaic Times to the End of the Peloponnesian War*. 2nd edn. Cambridge and New York.

Foucault, M. (1973) *The Birth of the Clinic: an archaeology of medical perception*. Tr. A. M. Sheridan Smith. London. Originally published in 1963 as *Naissance de la clinique*. Paris.

(1979) *The History of Sexuality I: an introduction*. Tr. R. Hurley. London. Originally published in 1976 as *Histoire de sexualité I: la volonté de savoir*. Paris.

(1985) *The Hisotry of Sexuality II: the use of pleasure*. Tr. R. Hurley. London. Originally published in 1984 as *Histoire de sexualité II: l'usage des plaisirs*. Paris.

(1986) *The History of Sexuality III. The care of the self*. Tr. R. Hurley. London. Originally published in 1984 as *Histoire de sexualité III: le souci de soi*. Paris.

Foxhall, L. (1989) 'Household, gender and property in classical Athens', *Classical Quarterly* 39: 22–44.

(1994) 'Pandora unbound: a feminist critique of Foucault's *History of Sexuality*', in N. Lindesfarne-Tapper and A. Cornwall, eds., *Dislocating Masculinity: comparative ethnographies*: 133–46. London.

(1995) 'Monumental ambitions: the significance of posterity in ancient Greece', in Spencer 1995: 132–49.

(1998) 'Natural sex: the attribution of sex and gender to plants in ancient Greece', in Foxhall and Salmon 1998a: 56–70.

(1999) 'Foreign powers: Plutarch and discourses of domination in Roman Greece', in S. Pomeroy, ed. *Plutarch on Women and Marriage*: 138–50. Oxford and New York.

(2000) 'The running sands of time: archaeology and the short-term', *World Archaeology* 31: 484–98.

(2002a) 'Access to resources in classical Greece: the egalitarianism of the polis in practice', in Cartledge *et al.* 2002: 209–20.

(2002b) 'Social control, Roman power and Greek politics in the world of Plutarch', in D. Cohen, ed., *Demokratie, Recht und soziale Kontrolle im klassischen Athen*: 173–88. Munich.

(2007a) *Olive Cultivation in Ancient Greece: seeking the ancient economy*. Oxford.

(2007b) 'House clearance: unpacking the kitchen in classical Greece', in Westgate *et al.* 2007: 233–42. London.

Graeber, D. (2011) 'Consumption', *Current Anthropology* 52: 489–511.

Graf, F. (1997) *Magic in the Ancient World*. Cambridge, MA.

Grimal, P., ed. (1974) *Histoire mondiale de la femme*. Paris.

Hales, S. (2003) *The Roman House and Social Identity*. Cambridge.

Hall, E. (1989) *Inventing the Barbarian: Greek self-definition through tragedy*. Oxford.

Hallett, C. H. (2005) *The Roman Nude: heroic portrait statuary 200 BC–AD 300*. Oxford and New York.

Hallett, J. (1984) *Fathers and Daughters in Roman Society: women and the elite family*. Princeton.

Halperin, D. M. (1990) *One Hundred Years of Homosexuality*. London and New York.

Halperin, D. M., Winkler, J. J. and Zeitlin, F. I., eds. (1990) *Before Sexuality: the construction of erotic experience in the ancient Greek world*. Princeton.

Hanson, A. E. (1990) 'The medical writers' woman', in Halperin *et al.* 1990: 309–38.

(1991) 'Continuity and change: three case studies in Hippocratic gynaecological therapy and theory', in Pomeroy 1991: 73–110.

Harders, A.-C. (2008) *Suavissima Soror: Untersuchungen zu den Bruder-Schwester-Beziehungen in der römischen Republik*. Munich.

Hardwick, L. (1990) 'Ancient Amazons: heroes, outsiders or women?', *Greece and Rome* 37: 14–36.

Harlow, M. (Forthcoming) *Roman Dress*. Cambridge.

Harlow, M and Larsson Loven, L. (2011) *Families in the Imperial and Late Antique Roman Worlds*. London.

Harlow, M. and Laurence, R. (2002) *Growing up and Growing Old in Ancient Rome*. London and New York.

Harris, E. (2002) 'Workshop, marketplace and household: the nature of technical specialization in classical Athens and its influence on economy and society', in Cartledge *et al.* 2002: 67–99.

Harris, W. V. (1982) 'The theoretical possibility of extensive infanticide in the Graeco-Roman world', *Classical Quarterly* 32: 114–16.

(1994) 'Child-exposure in the Roman Empire', *Journal of Roman Studies* 84: 1–22.

Harrison, A. R. W. (1968) *The Law of Athens I: family and property*. Oxford.

Harrison, J. (1894) 'Athene Ergane', *Classical Review* 8: 270–1.

(1900) 'Pandora's box', *Journal of Hellenic Studies* 20: 99–114.

(1965) 'Reminiscences of a student's life', *Arion* 4: 312–46.

Hawhee, D. (2004) *Bodily Arts: rhetoric and athletics in ancient Greece*. Austin, TX.

Hemelrijk, E. (2004) 'City patronesses in the Roman empire', *Historia* 53: 209–45.

(2007) 'Local empresses: priestesses of the imperial cult in the cities of the Latin West', *Phoenix* 61: 318–49.

(2008) 'Patronesses and "mothers" of Roman *collegia*', *Classical Antiquity* 27: 115–62.

(2009) 'Women and sacrifice in the Roman empire', in O. Hekster, S. Schmidt-Hofner and C. Witschel, eds., *Ritual Dynamics and Religious Change in the Roman Empire*: 253–67. Leiden and Boston.

Henderson, J. (1987) 'Older women in Attic comedy', *Transactions of the American Philological Association* 117: 105–29.

Hersch, K. (2010) *The Roman Wedding: ritual and meaning in antiquity*. Cambridge.

Hodkinson, S. (1986) 'Land tenure and inheritance in classical Sparta', *Classical Quarterly* 36: 378–406.

(2000) *Property and Wealth in Classical Sparta*. London.

Holford-Strevens, L. (2003) *Aulus Gellius: an Antonine scholar and his achievement*. Rev. edn. Oxford.

Hope, V. and Huskinson, J., eds. (2011) *Memory and Mourning: studies on Roman death*. Oxford and Oakville, CT.

Hopkins, K. (1980) 'Brother–sister marriage in Roman Egypt', *Comparative Studies in Society and History* 22: 303–54.

Hoy, D., ed. (1986) *Foucault: a critical reader*. Oxford.

Huebner, S. (2007) '"Brother–sister" marriage in Roman Egypt: a curiosity of humankind or a widespread family strategy?', *Journal of Roman Studies* 97: 21–49.

Humphreys, S. C. (1993) *The Family, Women and Death*. Rev. edn. London.

Hunt, A. S. and Edgar, C. C. (1932) *Select Papyri 1*. London and Cambridge, MA.

Hunt, P. (2007) 'Military forces', in Sabin *et al.* 2007, vol. 1: 108–46.

Huntley, K. (2010) 'Identifying children's graffiti in Roman Campania: a developmental psychological approach', in J. Baird and C. Taylor, eds., *Ancient Graffiti in Context*: 69–89. New York and London.

Hurwit, J. (1999) *The Athenian Acropolis*. Cambridge.

Huskinson, J. (1996) *Roman Children's Sarcophagi: their decoration and its social significance*. Oxford.

Jaggar, A. and Young, I., eds. (2000) *A Companion to Feminist Philosophy*. Malden, MA, and Oxford.

Jameson, M. (1990a) 'Private space and the Greek city', in O. Murray and S. Price, eds., *The Greek City from Homer to Alexander*: 171–95. Oxford.

(1990b) 'Domestic space in the Greek city-state', in S. Kent, ed., *Domestic Architecture and the Use of Space*: 92–113. Cambridge.

Johnstone, S. (2003) 'Women, property and surveillance in classical Athens', *Classical Antiquity* 22: 247–74.

Jones, J. E., Sackett, L. H. and Graham, A. J. (1962) 'The Dema House in Attica', *Annual of the British School at Athens* 57: 75–114.

Jongman, W. (2007) 'The early Roman Empire: consumption', in Morris *et al.* 2007: 592–617.

Kampen, N. (1981) *Image and Status: Roman working women in Ostia*. Berlin.

(2009) *Family Fictions in Roman Art*. Cambridge.

Keane, W. (2005) 'Signs are not the garb of meaning: on the social analysis of material things', in Miller 2005: 1–50.

Kennell, N. (1995) *The Gymnasium of Virtue: education and culture in ancient Sparta*. Chapel Hill, NC.

(2010) *The Spartans: a new history*. Oxford.

Keuls, E. (1985) *The Reign of the Phallus: sexual politics in ancient Athens*. Berkeley, Los Angeles and London.

King, H. (1998) *Hippocrates' Woman: reading the female body in ancient Greece*. London and New York.

Kleijwegt, M. (1991) *Ancient Youth: the ambiguity of youth and the absence of adolescence in Greco-Roman society*. Amsterdam.

Kleiner, D. (1987) *Roman Imperial Funerary Altars with Portraits*. Rome.

Knigge, U. (2005) *Der Bau Z*. Munich.

König, J. (2005) *Athletics and Literature in the Roman Empire*. Cambridge.

Kosmopoulou, A. (2001) '"Working women": female professionals on classical Attic gravestones', *Annual of the British School at Athens* 96: 281–319.

Küchler, S. (2005) 'Materiality and cognition: the changing face of things', in Miller 2005: 206–30.

Kunze, E. and Schleif, H. (1944) *Bericht über die Ausgrabungen in Olympia IV 1940 and 1941*. Berlin.

Kurke, L. (1992) 'The politics of ἁβροσύνη in archaic Greece', *Classical Antiquity* 11: 91–120.

Kyle, D. (1992) 'The Panathenaic Games: sacred and civic athletics', in Neils 1992b: 77–102.

(2007) *Sport and Spectacle in the Ancient World*. Oxford.

Lacey, W. (1968) *The Family in Classical Greece*. London.

Lambert, S. D. (1993) *The Phratries of Attica*. Ann Arbor, MI.

Langlands, R. (2006) *Sexuality Morality in Ancient Rome*. Cambridge.

Lanni, A. (2010) 'The expressive effect of the Athenian prostitution laws', *Classical Antiquity* 29: 45–67.

Lape, S. (2006) 'The psychology of prostitution in Aeschines' speech against Timarchus', in Faraone and McClure 2006: 139–60.

Laqueur, T. (1990) *Making Sex: body and gender from the Greeks to Freud*. Cambridge, MA.

Larmour, D., Miller, P. and Platter, C., eds. (1998) *Rethinking Sexuality: Foucault and classical antiquity*. Princeton.

Larson, J. (1995) *Greek Heroine Cults*. Madison, WI.

Laslett, P. (1977) *Family Life and Illicit Love in Earlier Generations*. Cambridge.

Laurence, R. (1994) *Roman Pompeii: space and society*. London.

Laurence, R. and Newsome, D., eds. (2011) *Rome, Ostia, Pompeii: movement and space*. Oxford.

Laurence, R. and Wallace-Hadrill, A., eds. (1997) *Domestic Space in the Roman World: Pompeii and beyond*. Portsmouth, RI.

Lawton, C. (2007) 'Children in classical Attic votive reliefs', in Cohen and Rutter 2007: 41–60.

Leader, R. E. (1997) ' In death not divided: gender, family and state on classical Athenian grave stelae', *American Journal of Archaeology* 101: 683–99.

Lee, Y.-L. (2010) 'Introduction: the politics of gender', in Y.-L. Lee, ed. *The Politics of Gender: a survey*. London and New York.

Lendon, J. E. (2007) 'War and society', in Sabin *et al.* 2007, vol. 1: 498–516.

Lewis, S. (2002) *The Athenian Woman: an iconographic handbook*. London and New York.

Lind, H. (1988) 'Ein Hetärentum am heiligen Tor?', *Museum Helveticum* 45: 158–69.

Linders, T. (1972) *Studies in the Treasure Records of Artemis Brauronia*. Stockholm.

Llewellyn-Jones, L. (2003) *Aphrodite's Tortoise: the veiled woman of ancient Greece*. Swansea.

Loman, P. (2004) 'No woman no war: women's participation in ancient Greek warfare', *Greece and Rome* 51: 34–54.

Lowe, N. (1998) 'Thesmophoria and Haloa: myth, physics and mysteries', in Blundell and Williamson 1998: 149–73.

Lynch, K. (2007) 'More thoughts on the space of the symposium', in Westgate *et al.* 2007: 243–50.

MacDowell, D. (1989) 'The *oikos* in Athenian law', *Classical Quarterly* 39: 10–21.

Mazarakis Ainian, A. (2007) 'Architecture and social structure in early iron age Greece', in Westgate *et al.* 2007: 157–68.

McGinn, T. (2002) 'Pompeian brothels and social history' in T. McGinn, P. Carafa, N. de Grummond, B. Bergmann and T. Najbjerg, eds., *Pompeian Brothels, Pompeii's Ancient History, Mirrors and Mysteries, Art and Nature at Oplontis, and the Herculaneum 'Basilica'*: 7-46. *Journal of Roman Archaeology* Suppl. 47. Portsmouth RI.

(2004) *The Economy of Prostitution in the Roman World*. Ann Arbor, MI.

ed. (2006) *Zoning Shame in the Roman City*. Madison, WI.

McNay, L. (1992) *Foucault and Feminism: power, gender and the self*. Cambridge.

McWilliam, J. (2001) 'Children among the dead: the influence of urban life on the commemoration of children on tombstone inscriptions', in Dixon 2001: 74–98.

Meskell, L. (1995) 'Goddesses, Gimbutas and "new age" archaeology', *Antiquity* 69: 74–86.

Mette-Dittmann, A. (1991) *Die Ehegesetze des Augustus*. Stuttgart.

Millender, E. (1999) 'Athenian ideology and the empowered Spartan woman', in S. Hodkinson and A. Powell, eds., *Sparta: new perspectives*: 355–91. London and Swansea.

Miller, D., ed. (2005) *Materiality*. Durham, NC, and London.

Miller, S. (2004) *Ancient Greek Athletics*. New Haven and London.

Miller, W. (1913) *Cicero: de Officiis*. Cambridge, MA.

Mills, H. (1984) 'Greek clothing regulations: sacred and profane?', *Zeitschrift für Papyrologie und Epigraphik* 55: 255–65.

Milnor, K. (2005) *Gender, Domesticity and the Age of Augustus*. Oxford and New York.

Montserrat, D., ed. (1998) *Changing Bodies, Changing Meanings: studies on the human body in antiquity*. London and New York.

Morgan, J. (2010) *The Classical Greek House*. Bristol.

Morgan, S., ed. (2006) *The Feminist History Reader*. London and New York.

Morris, I. (1998) 'Remaining invisible: the archaeology of the excluded in classical Athens', in S. Joshel and S. Murnaghan (eds), *Women and Slaves in
Greco-Roman Culture*: 193–220. London.

   (1999) 'Archaeology and gender ideologies in early archaic Greece', *Transactions
of the American Philological Association* 129: 305–17. Repr. in Golden and
Toohey 2003: 264–75.

   (2000) *Archaeology and Cultural History: words and things in Iron Age Greece*.
Malden, MA, and Oxford.

Morris, I., Saller, R. and Scheidel, W., eds. (2007) *The Cambridge Economic
History of the Greco-Roman World*. Cambridge.

Mullins, P. (2011) 'The archaeology of consumption', *Annual Review of
Anthropology* 40: 133–44.

Munson, R. V. (1988) 'Artemesia in Herodotus', *Classical Antiquity* 7: 91–4.

Neils, J. (1992a) 'Introduction', in Neils 1992b: 13–27.

   ed. (1992b) *Goddess and Polis: the Panathenaic festival in ancient Athens*.
Princeton.

Neils, J. and Oakley, J. H., eds. (2003) *Coming of Age in Ancient Greece: images of
childhood from the classical past*. New Haven and London.

Nevett, L. (1997) 'Perceptions of domestic space in Roman Italy', in Rawson and
Weaver 1997: 299–319.

   (1999) *House and Society in the Ancient Greek World*. Cambridge.

   (2010) *Domestic Space in Classical Antiquity*. Cambridge.

   (2011) 'Towards a female topography of the ancient Greek city: case studies for
late archaic and early classical Athens (*c.* 520–400 BCE)', *Gender & History*
23: 576–96.

Newby, Z. (2005) *Greek Athletics in the Roman World: victory and virtue*.
Oxford.

   (2006) *Athletics in the Ancient World*. Bristol.

Nielsen, I. (1993) *Thermae et Balnea*. 2 vols. Århus.

Oakley, J. H. (2004) *Picturing Death in Classical Athens*. Cambridge.

Oakley, J. H. and Sinos, R. H. (1993) *The Wedding in Ancient Athens*. Madison, WI.

Ogden, D. (1996) *Greek Bastardy*. Oxford.

Omitowoju, R. (2002) *Rape and the Politics of Consent in Classical Athens*.
Cambridge.

Orlandini, P. and Adamesteanu, D. (1960) 'Gela: nuovi scavi: l'impianto greco
do bagni pubblici presso "Ospizio"', *Notizie degli Scavi di Antichità* 14:
181–202.

Orlin, E. (2002) 'Foreign cults in Republican Rome: rethinking the Pomerial
rule', *Memoirs of the American Academy in Rome* 47: 1–18.

   (2008) 'Octavian and Egyptian cults: redrawing the boundaries of Romanness',
American Journal of Philology 129: 231–53.

Osborne, R. (1993) 'Women and sacrifice in classical Greece', *Classical Quarterly*
43: 392–405.

(2004) 'The object of dedication', *World Archaeology* 36: 1–10.

(2011) *The History Written on the Classical Greek Body*. Cambridge.

Osiek, C. (2008) 'Roman and Christian burial practices and the patronage of women', in Brink and Green 2008: 243–70.

Parker, H. (2004) 'Why were the Vestals virgin? Or the chastity of women and the safety of the Roman state', *American Journal of Philology* 125: 563–601.

Parker, R. (1996) *Athenian Religion: a history*. Oxford.

Parkin, T. (1992) *Demography and Roman Society*. Baltimore and London.

Patterson, C. (1985) '"Not worth the rearing": the causes of infant exposure in ancient Greece', *Transactions of the American Philological Association* 115: 103–23.

(1990) 'Those Athenian bastards', *Classical Antiquity* 9: 40–73.

(1991) 'Marriage and the married woman in Athenian law', in Pomeroy 1991: 48–72.

(1998) *The Family in Greek History*. Cambridge, MA, and London.

Percy, W. (1996) *Pederasty and Pedagogy in Archaic Greece*. Urbana, IL, and London.

Phang, S. (2008) *Roman Military Service: ideologies of discipline in the late Republic and early Principate*. Cambridge.

Pinney, C. (2005) 'Things happen: or, from which moment does that object come?', in Miller 2005: 256–72.

Pomeroy, S. (1973) 'Selected bibliography on women in antiquity', *Arethusa* 6: 127–57.

(1975) *Goddesses, Whores, Wives and Slaves: women in classical antiquity*. New York.

(1986) 'Copronyms and the exposure of infants in Egypt', in R. S. Bagnall and W. V. Harris, eds., *Studies in Roman Law in Memory of A. Arthur Schiller*: 147–62. Leiden.

ed. (1991) *Women's History and Ancient History*. Chapel Hill, NC, and London.

(1993) 'Infanticide in Hellenistic Greece', in A. Cameron and A. Kuhrt, eds., *Images of Women in Antiquity*: 207–22. Rev. edn. London.

(1997) *Families in Classical and Hellenistic Greece*. Oxford.

(2002) *Spartan Women*. Oxford.

Pritchett, W. K. (1956) 'The Attic stelae, part 2', *Hesperia* 25: 178–328.

Rabinow, P., ed. (1984) *The Foucault Reader*. Harmondsworth.

Radice, B. (1969) *Pliny, Letters and Panegyricus*. Cambridge, MA.

Raditsa, L. F. (1980) 'Augustus' legislation concerning marriage, procreation, love affairs and adultery', *Aufstieg und Niedergang des Römisches Welt* II 13: 278–339.

Ramsey, G. (2011) 'The queen and the city: royal female intervention and patronage in Hellenistic civic communities', *Gender & History* 23: 510–27.

Rawson, B. (1999) 'Education, the Romans and us', *Antichthon* 33: 81–98.

(2003) *Children and Childhood in Roman Italy*. Oxford.

ed. (2011) *A Companion to Families in the Greek and Roman Worlds*. Chichester.

Rawson, B. and Weaver, P., eds. (1997) *The Roman Family in Italy: status, sentiment, space*. Oxford.

Remijsen, S. and Clarysse, W. (2008) 'Incest or adoption? Brother–sister marriage in Roman Egypt revisited', *Journal of Roman Studies* 98: 53–61.

Richardson, D., McLaughlin, J. and Casey, M., eds. (2006) *Intersections between Feminist and Queer Theory*. Basingstoke and New York.

Riddle, J. (1992) *Contraception and Abortion from the Ancient World to the Renaissance*. Cambridge, MA, and London.

(1997) *Eve's Herbs: a history of contraception and abortion in the West*. Cambridge, MA, and London.

Robinson, V. and Hockey, J. (2011) *Masculinities in Transition*. Basingstoke.

Roccos, L. (2000) 'Back-mantle and peplos: the special costume of Greek maidens in 4th-century funerary and votive reliefs', *Hesperia* 69: 235–65.

Rousselle, A. (1988) *Porneia: on desire and the body in antiquity*. Oxford.

Rowlandson, J. (1998) *Women and Society in Greek and Roman Egypt: a sourcebook*. Cambridge.

Rowlandson, J. and Takahashi, R. (2009) 'Brother–sister marriage and inheritance strategies in Greco-Roman Egypt', *Journal of Roman Studies* 99: 104–39.

Roy, J. (1997) 'An alternative sexuality for classical Athenians', *Greece and Rome* 44: 11–22.

Sabin, P. (2000) 'The face of Roman battle', *Journal of Roman Studies* 90: 1–17.

Sabin, P. and de Souza, P. (2007) 'Battle', in Sabin *et al.* 2007, vol. 1: 399–460.

Sabin, P., van Wees, H. and Whitby, M., eds. (2007) *The Cambridge History of Greek and Roman Warfare*. 2 vols. Cambridge.

Saller, R. (1984) 'Roman dowry and the devolution of property in the Principate', *Classical Quarterly* 34: 195–205.

(1994) *Patriarchy, Property and Death in the Roman Family*. Cambridge.

(2007) 'Household and gender', in Morris *et al.* 2007: 87–112.

Saller, R. and Shaw, B. (1984) 'Tombstones and Roman family relations in the Principate: civilians, soldiers and slaves', *Journal of Roman Studies* 74: 124–56.

Scafuro, A. C. (1994) ' Witnessing and false witnessing: proving citizenship and kin identity in fourth century Athens', in A. L. Boegehold and A. C. Scafuro, eds., *Athenian Identity and Civic Ideology*: 156–98. Baltimore and London.

Scanlon, T. (1984) 'The footrace of the Heraia at Olympia', *Ancient World* 9: 77–90.

(1988) 'Virgineum Gymnasium', in W. Raschke, ed., *The Archaeology of the Olympics*: 185–216. Madison, WI.

(2002) *Eros and Greek Athletics*. Oxford.

Schaps, D. (1979) *Economic Rights of Women in Ancient Greece*. Edinburgh.

(1982) 'The women of Greece in wartime', *Classical Philology* 77: 193–213.

(1998) 'What was free about a free Athenian woman?', *Transactions of the American Philological Association* 128: 161–88.

Scheid, J. (1991) 'D'indispensables étrangères: les rôles religieux des femmes à Rome', in P. Schmitt Pantel, ed., *Histoire des femmes en Occident 1: l'antiquité*: 405–37. Paris.

Scheidel, W. (1995) 'The most silent women of Greece and Rome: rural labour and women's life in the ancient world (I)', *Greece and Rome* 42: 202–17.

(1996a) *Measuring Sex, Age and Death in the Roman Empire: explorations in ancient demography*. Ann Arbor, MI.

(1996b) 'The most silent women of Greece and Rome: rural labour and women's life in the ancient world (II)', *Greece and Rome* 43: 1–10.

(2001a) 'Progress and problems in Roman demography', in Scheidel, 2001b: 1–82.

ed. (2001b) *Debating Demography*. Leiden, Boston and Cologne.

Schultz, C. E. (2000) 'Modern prejudice and ancient praxis: female worship of Hercules at Rome', *Zeitschrift für Papyrologie und Epigraphik* 133: 291–7.

(2006) *Women's Religious Activity in the Roman Republic*. Chapel Hill, NC.

Scott, E. (1999) *The Archaeology of Infancy and Infant Death*. Oxford.

(2000) 'Unpicking a myth: the infanticide of female and disabled infants in antiquity', in G., Davies, A., Gardner and K., Lockyear eds., *TRAC 2000: proceedings of the Tenth Annual Theoretical Roman Archaeology Conference*: 143–51. Oxford.

Scott, J. (1986) 'Gender: a useful category of historical analysis', *American Historical Review* 91: 1053–75.

Scott, M. (2012) *Space and Society in the Greek and Roman Worlds*. Cambridge.

(2013) 'The spatial indeterminacy and social life of Greek athletic facilities (other than stadia)', in P. Christesen and D. Kyle, eds., *Companion to Ancient Sport and Spectacle*. Oxford.

Seltman, C. (1956) *Women in Antiquity*. London.

Serrati, J. (2007) 'Warfare and the state', in Sabin *et al.* 2007, vol. 1: 461–97. Cambridge.

Serwint, N. (1993) 'The female athletic costume at the Heraia and prenuptial initiation rites', *American Journal of Archaeology* 97: 403–22.

Shapiro, H. (1991) 'The iconography of mourning in Athenian art', *American Journal of Archaeology* 95: 629–56.

Shaw, B. (1984) 'Latin funerary epigraphy and family life in the later Roman Empire', *Historia* 33: 457–97.

(1987) 'The age of Roman girls at marriage, some reconsiderations', *Journal of Roman Studies* 77: 30–46.

(2001) 'Raising and killing children: two Roman myths', *Mnemosyne* 54: 31–77.

Shaw, B. and Saller, R. (1984) 'Close-kin marriage in Roman society?', *Man* 19: 432–44.

Shipley, F. (1924) *Velleius Paterculus, Res Gestae Divi Augusti*. Cambridge, MA.

Showden, C. (2009) 'What's political about the new feminisms?', *Frontiers: A Journal of Women's Studies* 30: 166–98.

Sissa, G. (1990) 'Maidenhood without maidenhead: the female body in ancient Greece', in Halperin *et al.* 1990: 339–64.

Smith, C. (2006) *The Roman Clan: the gens from ancient ideology to modern anthropology*. Cambridge.

Spencer, N., ed. (1995) *Time, Tradition and Society in Greek Archaeology: bridging the great divide*. London.

Staples, A. (1998) *From Good Goddess to Vestal Virgins: sex and category in Roman religion*. London.

Stears, K. (1995) 'Dead women's society: constructing female gender in classical Athenian funerary sculpture', in Spencer 1995: 109–29.

Steiner, D. (1993) 'Pindar's "oggetti parlanti"', *Harvard Studies in Classical Philology* 95: 159–80.

Stern, Y. (2000) 'The testamentary phenomenon in ancient Rome', *Historia* 49: 413–28.

Sullivan, J. (1973) 'Editorial', *Arethusa* 6: 5–6.

Sutton, R. (2004) 'Family portraits: recognizing the "oikos" on Attic red-figure pottery', in A. Chapin, ed., *XAPIΣ: essays in honor of Sara A. Immerwahr*: 327–50. Princeton.

Takács, S. (2000) 'Politics and religion in the Bacchanalian affair of 186 BCE', *Harvard Studies in Classical Philology* 100: 301–10.

   (2008) *Vestal Virgins, Sibyls and Matrons: women in Roman religion*. Austin, TX.

Tanner, J. (2000) 'Portraits, power and patronage in the late Roman Republic', *Journal of Roman Studies* 90: 18–50.

   (2001) 'Nature, culture and the body in classical Greek religious art', *World Archaeology* 33: 257–76.

Tarlow, S. (2011) *Ritual, Belief and the Dead in Early Modern Britain and Ireland*. Cambridge.

Thomas, C. (1973) 'Matriarchy in early Greece: the bronze and dark ages', *Arethusa* 6: 173–95.

Thomas, R. (1989) *Oral Tradition and Written Record in Classical Athens*. Cambridge.

Thompson, H. and Wycherley, R. (1972) *The Agora of Athens* (The Athenian Agora XIV). Princeton.

Thompson, L. (2010) *The Role of the Vestal Virgins in Roman Civic Religion: a structuralist study of the crimen incesti*. Lewiston, NY, and Lampeter.

Thomson, G. (1949) *Studies in Ancient Greek Society*. London.

Tierney, J. (1947) 'The "Senatus Consultum de Bacchanalibus"', *Proceedings of the Royal Irish Academy: Section C: Archaeology, Celtic Studies, History, Linguistics, Literature* 51: 89–117.

Todd, S. C. (1993) *The Shape of Athenian Law*. Oxford.

Treggiari, S. (1991) *Roman Marriage*. Oxford.

Trimble, J. (2011) *Women and Visual Replication in Roman Imperial Art and Culture*. Cambridge.

Tsiolis, V. (2001) 'Las termas de Fregellae: arquetectura, technologia y cultura balnear en el Lacio durante los siglos III y II a. C.', *Cuadernos de Prehistoria y Arquelogia de la Universidad Autonomia de Madrid* 27: 85–114.

Tsoukala, V. (2009) 'Honorary shares of sacrificial meat in Attic vase painting', *Hesperia* 78: 1–40.

van Bremen, R. (1996) *The Limits of Participation: women and civic life in the Greek East in the Hellenistic and Roman periods*. Amsterdam.

van Nortwick, T. (2008) *Imagining Men: ideals of masculinity in ancient Greek culture*. Westport, CT, and London.

van Wees, H. (2004) *Greek Warfare: myths and realities*. London.

(2007) 'War and society', in Sabin *et al.* 2007, vol. 1: 273–99.

Vernant, J.-P. (1991) *Mortals and Immortals: collected essays*. Princeton.

Versnel, H. (1992) 'The festival for Bona Dea and the Thesmophoria', *Greece and Rome* 39: 31–55.

Veyne, P. (1982) 'L'homosexualité à Rome', *Communications* 35: 26–33.

(1985) 'Homosexuality in ancient Rome', in P. Aries and A. Béjin, eds., *Western Sexuality: practice and precept in past and present times*: 26–35. Oxford.

Vidal-Naquet, P. (1986) *The Black Hunter: forms of thought and forms of society in the Greek world*. Baltimore.

Wace, A. J. B. (1929) 'The lead figurines', in Dawkins 1929: 249–84.

Wacker, C. (1996) *Das Gymnasion in Olympia: Geschichte und Funktion*. Würzburg.

Walker, S. (1983) 'Women and housing in classical Greece', in A. Cameron and A. Kuhrt, eds., *Images of Women in Antiquity*: 81–91. Rev. edn. London and New York.

(1995) *Greek and Roman Portraits*. London.

Wallace-Hadrill, A. (1981) 'Family and inheritance in the Augustan marriage laws', *Proceedings of the Cambridge Philological Society* 27: 58–80.

(1994) *Houses and Society in Pompeii and Herculaneum*. Princeton.

(1995) 'Public honour and private shame: the urban texture of Pompeii', in T. Cornell and K. Lomas, eds., *Urban Society in Roman Italy*: 39–62. New York and London.

Walsh, P. (1996) 'Making a drama out of a crisis: Livy on the Bacchanalia', *Greece and Rome* 43: 188–203.

Walter, N. (2010) *Living Dolls: the return of sexism*. London.

Ward, R. B. (1992) 'Women in Roman baths', *Harvard Theological Review* 85: 125–47.

Watson, K. (2005) 'Queer theory', *Group Analysis* 38: 67–81.

Westgate, R., Fisher, N. and Whitley, J. eds. (2007) *Building Communities: house settlement and society in the Aegean and beyond*. London.

Whelehan, I. (2007) *Modern Feminist Thought*. Edinburgh.

Whitehead, D. (1986) *The Demes of Attica, 508/7–ca. 250 BC*. Princeton.

Wildfang, R. (2006) *Rome's Vestal Virgins: a study of Rome's Vestal priestesses in the late Republic and early Empire*. London and New York.

Willetts, R. F. (1967) *The Law Code of Gortyn*. Berlin.

Williams, C. A. (2010) *Roman Homosexuality: ideologies of masculinity in classical antiquity*. 2nd edn. New York and Oxford.

Wilson, A. (2006) 'Practically between post-menopause and post-modern', in D. Richardson, J. McLaughlin and M. Casey, eds., *Intersections between Feminist and Queer Theory*: 156–73. Basingstoke and New York.

Winkler, J. (1990a) 'The constraints of desire: erotic magical spells', in J. Winkler, *The Constraints of Desire: the anthropology of sex and gender in ancient Greece*: 71–98. London and New York.

(1990b) 'Laying down the law: the oversight of men's sexual behaviour in classical Athens', in J. Winkler, *The Constraints of Desire: the anthropology of sex and gender in ancient Greece*: 45–70. London and New York.

Wiseman, T. (1998) *Roman Drama and Roman History*. Exeter.

Woodward, A. M. (1929) 'The inscriptions', in Dawkins 1929: 285–377.

Woolf, G. (2009) 'Found in translation: the religion of the Roman diaspora', in O. Hekster, S. Schmidt-Hofner and C. Witschel, eds., *Ritual Dynamics and Religious Change in the Roman Empire*: 239–52. Leiden and Boston.

Worthington, I. (2006) *Demosthenes, Speeches 60 and 61, Prologues, Letters.* Austin, TX.

Wrenhaven, K. (2009) 'The identity of the "woolworkers" in the Attic manumissions', *Hesperia* 78: 367–86.

Wrigley, E. A. (1997) *English Population History from Family Reconstitution, 1580–1837*. Cambridge.

Wyke, M., ed. (1998a) *Parchments of Gender: deciphering the body in antiquity.* Oxford.

ed. (1998b) *Gender and the Body in the Ancient Mediterranean*. Oxford.

ed. (2002) *The Roman Mistress: ancient and modern representations*. Oxford.

Yegül, F. (2010) *Bathing in the Roman World*. Cambridge.

Young, R. S. (1951) 'Sepulturae intra urbem', *Hesperia* 20: 67–134.

Index